T0114933

Thorns And Roses
A Play

Frida M. Mbunda-Nekang

Langaa Research & Publishing CIG
Mankon, Bamenda

Publisher

Langaa RPCIG
Langaa Research & Publishing Common Initiative Group
P.O. Box 902 Mankon
Bamenda
North West Region
Cameroon
Langaagrp@gmail.com
www.langaa-rpcig.net

Distributed in and outside N. America by African Books Collective
orders@africanbookscollective.com
www.africanbookscollective.com

ISBN-10: 9956-763-23-3

ISBN-13: 978-9956-763-23-8

Dedication

This play is dedicated to my children who because of their origin must never give up for there are always thorns in roses

Foreword

When a pen which drips woman, academic, mother, wife, teacher and administrator proposes to visit the stage, we expect the product to be as complex as the person. And we will be entirely justified in our expectation given that the stage more often than not is that place which captures and dramatizes our core selves in all their complexity. How often did those who knew Bate Besong (BB) exclaim on meeting the man: "How he looks like his plays!" Even the white-haired Soyinka, does he too not put the same feelings in us? Knowledge of the author is always a good thing: it enriches our knowledge of the product and impacts our way of coping with it. "Thorns and Roses" is produced by just that kind of pen. But in spite of her multi-layered identity, Frida Mbunda has succeeded in writing a play whose greatest attractions lie in its unassuming, down-to-earth appeal. It is the story of a single-parent home where a mother dedicates her life to her loving but vulnerable single daughter.

As its title suggests, the play employs the allegorical archetype to colour the stage with characters and issues of immediate relevance. This is just what the Canadian playwright Garrison Keller does in "Prodigal Son", a play built after its biblical example and used to warn against the dangers of unchecked filial idiosyncrasies.

Womanhood is at the centre of Mbunda's dramatic quest. She knows that being a woman means being exposed to the attractions of shortcuts to happiness. Such harmful options are proposed in the play by the likes of the Inspector Jerome, the Inspector of Education who seduces and impregnates Noyen, the central girl character, thereby disrupting her education. But the play does not for that matter fall into the threadbare danger of militant feminism. Rather, it summons the sedate resources of motherhood, incarnated by Noyen's mother, to whether the storm of the girl's escapades and other male misdeeds in the village. It is for this reason that when Kamsi schemes to have his rival Lobte's school shut down, the women resolve to challenge the move by activating the Febien, the women's cult which wields extensive powers. But before they do so their leader cautions: "Remember we are good wives and must respect our husbands and Mr. Kamsi is one of them."

Like the balanced hand she is, Mbunda knows that societal values are not determined by a Manichean gender opposition in which one category is the roses and another the thorns. Harm is the work not solely of lustful men; it is just as likely to be engineered by young girls. For instance, Yune, Noyen's classmate, does everything to push the hesitant Noyen into the waiting hands of the Mr. Jerome Inspector Education. Every gender, the play seems to be opining, has its thorns and roses; every positive situation its flipside. The HOD of Law, for instance, is everything Inspector Jerome is not. The former is fatherly and supportive of Noyen where the latter sees her only as an object to be used and discarded. The boys, practically without exception, cut endearing figures, with their strong concern for the welfare of their female mates. In fact at the end of the play all the young men and women bond through marriage and professional ascendancy into an exclusive class of successful businessmen/women and intellectuals.

"Thorns and Roses" is a light-hearted, optimistic entertainment piece with no claims to recondite intellectuality, but with legitimate claims to social relevance. It winds up on the decision of the friends' guild to start a fund for the development of their village and the education of the girl child.

Viewed against the background of today's world and its moral excesses, Mbunda's production earns a place among the efforts that speak to the core concerns of the moment; and in a lasting way.

Professor George Nyamndi

Characters

Nchindah Noyen
Mnkong Peter
Nene Buji
Yaya
Nchioh
Babey Maih
Yune
Noyen's mother
Nchioh's mother
Mr. Kamsi
Principal
Inspector Jerome
Inspector Caleb
Maih
Febien (Members of the women's cult)

Act one

Scene I

(Noyen's home, a small room consisting of a bed a chair and a few items. Her mother, an average age women dresses in traditional attire sits at the corner of the bed and is doing some needle work)

Mother: Noyen!, Noyen!, Noyen oh! Where has this child gone to? *(Pauses)*

Noyen: Yes Mother. I am coming. *(she hurries in)*

Mother: Where have you been? I have been calling for the past five minutes.

Noyen: When I finished cooking, I took some food to Pa Ngum *(she examines her mother's work)*. This design is so beautiful. I wish I could do it.

Mother: You have shown no interest in it since I started making it, however, I will teach you. (Pauses)That is not why I called you anyway. I want to discuss your education.

Noyen: *(Surprised)* what about my education Mama?

Mother: *(Calmly)* You know I cannot afford to send you out of this village for further studies, so get as much education as you can from our lone village school.

Noyen: *(Proudly)* Mother, you know I am very prepared to study so as to work and improve on our standard of living.

Mother: I know that my daughter and I am praying that more schools and higher institutions of learning be establish in this village so that many of our children will have a chance to be trained so as to gain employment and improve on our conditions of living.

Noyen: *(expressing doubt)* Mama, I wish your prayer will be answered, but with the kind of elites we have in this village I do not see the possibility *(pauses)*. If you can remember, when Mr. Kamsi started Kamsi Comprehensive College, the lone college in this village, many of our politician, those we all count on and those we called elites did everything to have the college closed down. *(Pauses again and then speaks contemplatively and slowly)*At times I laugh at the ignorance of the villagers. They are easily deceived by propaganda. *(Pauses)*Do you know what Pa Ngum told me when I went to give him food?

Mother: *(Getting interested)* No my daughter. What did he say?

Noyen: He talked about the Lumito political rally that took place on Ngosine. He said since this village was founded by Mnkong Moteh it has never known famine, but when this group which calls itself the Poisants was founded, famine came to the land and the people now live in misery. He showed me some soap and rice that was distributed to them at the rally and said he will no longer send Maih to secondary school as he had planned, because the chairperson of the Lumito party told them that the Poisants, that have brought so much misery to this land are mainly intellectuals. He said that education makes children rebellious and a danger to the nation.

Mother: *(Angrily)* That is rubbish *(pauses)* he will regret his decision.

Noyen: He is so fearful because, Maih as he says is the most assertive of his daughters, a quality he says places her at a disadvantage. Sending her to college he believes will only make her situation worse.

Mother: *(Emphatically)* What else did he tell you?

Noyen: He said the chairman of the Lumito party told them that Government school which was promised to us during the campaign will no longer be granted because the Poisants have written against it.

Mother: (Surprised) What! That the government school will not be granted? *(pauses)* I had hoped that like in other villages, we will be able to send our children to school free of charge.

Noyen: *(mockingly)* Free of charge. Hmm *(pauses)* That is where you go wrong again Mama. When the government grants a school, it is the parents who construct the classrooms and even pay most of the teachers. Often, our wily politicians use the opportunity to exploit the poor and enrich themselves. Remember, when the government primary school in Beih was granted. Parents were forced to pay a thousand francs before their children were allowed to sit just for the interview.

Mother: *(Disappointed)* what do you think we can do my daughter? *(slowly)* I know our ancestor will save us.

Noyen: *(slowly)* Our ancestors. *(Pauses)* At times I think our ancestors have abandoned us.

Mother: *(Emphatically)* Our ancestors will never abandon us as long as we are bound to them.

Noyen: *(Cutting in)* True Mother, but are we bound to them? Everyone in Kale wants to live like a white. The hospitality, the love and oneness that reigned in the days of our ancestors has been thrown to the dogs. What we have is greed, jealousy, hatred, violence, selfishness and blackmailing. Our leaders and our youths have given up on our culture and the efforts of our mothers to restore our tradition are in vain. What hope is there in a government and in youths whose motto is "you chop, me self I chop, palaver finish"? Those who are fortunate to have the juicy morsel in their mouths have their teeth too tight that nothing drops.

Mother: It is a convoluted situation and the solution cannot be provided in a day or by an individual; that is why we, the mothers of this village advocate for unity, hard work and honesty, values that kept us together in the past.

Noyen: *(Nodding her head)* Unity hard work and honesty, Yes, these virtues kept our ancestors together *(light fades)*.

Scene II

(At Kamsi Comprehensive College, Inspector Jerome: the Inspector of Education is present for a prize giving ceremony. The Inspector and principal enter the hall and students stand and greet)

Students: Good Morning Sir, Welcome to Kamsi Comprehensive College. Our Moto is Knowledge, integrity and Prosperity.

Principal: Remain standing as the band leads us in the singing of the national anthem.

Anthem   The four way test of the things we think, say and do
(S:- d:- m:- s- m:.m:- s:--
Is it the truth? Is it the truth?
s:-s.s.s s:-s.s.s
Will it bring Good will and better friendship?
s:- d:- m:- s- m:.m:- s: m:---d
Will it be beneficial to all concern?
(Courtesy Rotary International)
s:- f:- m:- d- m:.d:- m:

(The anthem ends with a thunderous applause and all present sit down and the principal, a tall handsome man of middle age takes the floor).

Principal: His highness the Fon of Kale, the honourable Inspector of Education, our honourable parliamentarians, dear parents and the entire staff and students of Kamsi Comprehension College, the inspector whom we have been expecting since morning has finally arrived. (*Cheerfully to the Inspector*) You are welcome sir. It is an honour for us to have you in our midst. (*Back to students*) I hope you will be very attentive to the message he has for us. (*To the Inspector*) Over to you sir.

Inspector Jerome: His highness the Fon of Kale, honourable parliamentarians, distinguished guest, dear parents, staff and students of Kamsi Comprehensive College and the entire members of Kale community, good afternoon,

All: Good afternoon sir.

Inspector Jerome: I am very happy to be here today, but before I proceed, I want to apologize for coming late. The delay was due to the bad state of the road that links your village to the divisional headquarter, Now that I have seen the situation, I assured you that the road will be tarred in a couple of weeks (*Thunderous applause*). This school is well known both for its academic excellence and moral rectitude. Continue in the same spirit so as to be able to carry the mantle of leadership which we will surely handover to you. I wish to emphasize that each of you should be on the alert because there are many dreaded diseases and cultic groups in this global age that can cut short your dreams. Abide by what you are taught in this excellent college and your future will be secured. I congratulate in advance the students who will receive prizes today and encourage those who will not receive prizes to work hard next year so that they will receive prizes. *(Students clap as he hands over the microphone to the principal).*

Principal: Thank you very much sir. Students, I hope you will abide by our Inspector's counsel *(pauses)*. Due to the inspector's tied schedules, we will go directly to the prize giving ceremony. I will read the names of the students and the prizes will be given by our Inspectors. The first prize is the Minister of Education's prize for the best student in Mathematics and it goes to Mnkong Peter *(He receives the prize amidst cheers)*. The next prize is the honourable parliamentarian's prize for the best student in French. This prize goes to Babey Maih. His Royal Highness' prize for the best student in History goes to Nene Buji. *(she goes for the prize amidst applauds)*. The prize for the best student in Biology goes to Dumse Ngek *(many other prizes are given)*. The last prize is the Prime Minister's prize for the best all round student in this college. This prize goes to Noyen Nchinda *(Noyen goes for the prize amidst great applause from the students. Inspector Jerome is lost in admiration of Noyen's beauty. He holds the prize a little longer than is necessary, recovers suddenly and hands the prize to Noyen. The principal and the others present expressed surprised at his behaviour)*.

Principal: We have come to the end of the prize giving ceremony. The Inspector will make the closing remark.

Inspector Jerome: I once again congratulate all the students who have received prizes today and encourage parents to do all in their power to send their children to school because knowledge is power. I want to end this prize giving ceremony by making a donation of three new classrooms *(applause)*. I will also have a working session with teachers to discuss ways to improve their working conditions.

Principal: Let us stand and sing the Farewell song before our Inspector leaves. Mnkong Peter goes out from the crowd and tunes the song and all the students join in the singing

Mnkong: We are the students of Kamsi College, Kamsi College, Kamsi College. We are the students of Kamsi College, we wish to say farewell to you Our dear Inspector is going away, going away, going away
Our dear Inspector is going away
Goodbye Papa, goodbye to you
Goodbye Papa, goodbye to you.

(The students continued standing while the Inspector leaves with the principal. The guest leave and the students start discussing among themselves.

Nchioh: *(Enviously)* Congratulation Noyen. I wish your mother had come.

Noyen: You know my mother, she is always busy. If I had insisted, she would have attended but then, she will spend sleepless nights trying to make up for lost time.

Nchioh: I will work very hard next year so that I will be given a prize

Noyen: Ya, it is necessary. I want to be like my mother, strong independent and confident. As women how else can we be known except through hard work?

Yune: *(Cutting in)* Noyen, I disagree with you. Women can be known in other ways, not necessary through hard work.

Noyen: Yune, I am not in the mode to argue. I am going home. I am anxious to see the smile on my mother's face. *(She rushes out)*

Nchioh: *(Interested)* Yune, how else can women make it except through hard world? We need to work hard to convince our parents who believe that a women's place is in the kitchen to send more of our sisters to school.

Yune: A women is the crown of creation. If a woman works hard fine, if she does not work hard fine.

Nchioh: How do you mean?

Yune: You talk as if you do not know that our society wants just success. The end justifies the means. Look at Elvis Kesum who dropped out in form two, disappeared to the north and returned a few months later with a fleet of cars. The community hailed him as a successful man *(in a boastful manner)* Look at me, beautiful, fearful and wonderfully made; I can still make it without hard work.

Nchioh: *(Cuts in)* Yune, I have no time for an unfruitful discussion. *(She leaves)*

Yune: *(Following her)* You can all go to hell. Someday I will prove what I mean. (To herself)There is nowhere that hard work can take a woman to that my beauty will not take me. I can even go to places with my beauty that hard work can never take them. I am always a red rose that can never be resisted. *(She looks at her watch)* Wao! It is almost 3:00pm. Let me get home now so I can go early to the club tonight. *(She leaves)*

Scene III

(In town during Youth day celebration; Noyen is seen walking along the road. Inspector Jerome horns and stops his car. Noyen is surprised that he recognizes her)

Inspector Jerome: *(shouting and horning)* Hello girl! Hello girl! Hello girl!

Noyen: *(Recognizes him and genuflects to greet him)* Good afternoon sir.

Inspector Jerome: *(In a lively manner)* Good afternoon Noyen, You are such a well behaved girl. How is your principal?

Noyen: He is fine sir. Sir I am surprised you remembered my name.

Inspector Jerome: *(enthusiastically)* surprised? *(Calmly)* Why? Your name has been music to me since I heard it. Hop into the car let me give you a treat.

Noyen: *(Hesitating)* Mm mm mm, but sir, sir….

Inspector Jerome: I insist. I just want to show you how I appreciated well-mannered girls.

Noyen: Thank you very much sir, but I am on my way home.

Inspector Jerome: *(Expressing surprise)* Returning home? Today is youth day, your day and you want to take that beauty to the village so soon? Well, Let us share a drink in the bar over there. We won't be long.

Noyen: Sir, it is against our school rules to drink in bars.

Inspector Jerome: *(Angry to frighten her)* Child, I am the inspector of Education and I know the rules governing schools. I have a message for your principal and I want you to take it along. I know you are a student so I cannot take you to a public bar. *(Noyen enters the car suspiciously)*

Inspector Jerome: *(After they are seated in the private section of one of the renowned Rest houses in town)* How are studies my girl?

Noyen: *(Uneasy)* Ok sir.

Inspector Jerome: *(To Vendor)* Give us two bottles of top. (To Noyen) Study hard; things are very difficult these days. Now, you need not only pass but pass with distinction. *(Their drinks are brought and Noyen serves them and he proposed a toast)* Let us have a toast for love and you're your success in everything you do.

Noyen: *(A bit relaxed)* Things have really changed sir, we have just a handful of graduates in my village yet some go unemployed.

Inspector Jerome: *(Shifting towards her while she shifts away from him)* Call me Jelly. That will never be the case with you my Rose, for I will ensure that you have the best job this country can offer. I will give you everything you want. You will have nice dresses. You will go to nice places and you will study out of the village and even abroad if you wish.*(pauses and declares in a romantic manner)* Noyen, I fell in love with you when I saw you at the prize giving ceremony and I have been looking for an opportunity to tell you how much I love you. I hope you will not turn me down.

Noyen: *(Cuts in, getting irritated)* I will think about it.

Inspector Jerome: *(Firmly)* What is there to be thought about? *(angry)*You either decide to continue to move about in rags or become a queen and a model.

Noyen: *(Stands, really angry)* Sir, to have an affair is immoral, and whether I am in rags or a model does not bother me.

If you have forgotten your message for my principal I think I should be on my way.

Inspector Jerome: (*Stands too and tries to calm her down*) Please! Please, Noyen do not misunderstand me. You are a pretty girl even if you are in rags. I meant no harm. I just wanted to help you. Here is my card. Call on me at Room six of the Delegation of Education and the pleasure will be mine. Have this for your transport. (*Noyen hesitates but he pleads with her and she takes the money*) Let's go. (*They leave*).

Scene IV

(*At Kamsi Comprehensive College. Noyen enters, closely follow by Yune and Yaya*)

Yaya: Good morning Noyen. You disappeared in town and I got really worried when you did not call on me on your return.

Noyen: I was so tired. You know a journey on these roads always make one sick

Yune: The situation becomes worse each day. I wonder what the council in this village does (*pauses*) and to think that before one sells even a needle in the market, you are forced to pay a hundred minas. Where this money goes to, only our ancestors can tell.

Noyen: It is used to build private houses and to send wives and girlfriends on pleasures trips abroad, and then make empty promises. We are even lucky that the driver's union does some minor repairs. Things would have been worst.

Yaya: *(Resigned)* Forget about the roads. Let talk about the youth day. *(Mnkong arrives)*

Mnkong: Good day girls.

All: Mnkong, how was the youth day?

Mnkong: Youth day! What is youthful about the day? Is it the moral decadence that characterizes the day?

Yune: *(Getting angry)* Mnkong stop. Do not dampen my spirit. I had open doors on the youth day.

Mnkong: What do you mean by open doors?

Yaya: Mine was just normal.

Yune: Mine was more than normal. I had much fun and brought home many goodies.

All: Big baby, big baby.

Noyen: Mnkong, I am glad you are here. I love your sincerity and I hope you will be very sincere today. I have a problem, should I really call it a problem? Well, let me just say a story, I will tell you the story and I expect sincere answers to the questions I will ask afterward.

Yune: I hope it is an interesting story? I do not wish to be bored with morality tales.

Noyen: Do you remember the Inspector who presided over our prize giving ceremony last year?

Mnkong and Yaya: Yes we do.

Noyen: I saw him in town yesterday

Mnkong and Yaya: We saw him too!

Noyen: *(Unconcerned)* More than that, he gave me a drink and said he was crazy about me but I told him I will think about his proposal.

Yune: *(Wishfully)* Noyen, you are a lucky but foolish girl. If I were you, I would have accepted his proposal there and then. Imagine the nice things he will …

Mnkong: *(Cuts in angrily)* Nice things, *(Pauses)* What an advice to give to a friend *(Calmly to Noyen)* Noyen, do you think the inspector loves you? He has his family. He just wants to use you, to exploit your youth and your beauty and then laugh at you. Think of what will happen if you are caught and dismissed or if you get pregnant or contract one of the deadly diseases. Please, Noyen, please remain the good girl you are.

Noyen: Thanks Mnkong. I see with you and…

Yune: *(Cuts in Angrily)* See with him and continue to live in poverty *(she rushes out)*.

Mnkong: *(Angry)* Go away slot. Noyen, your friendship with Yune will land you in trouble. She is a negative influence. Keep away from her.

Noyen: Thank you Mnkong. I will see you later. Let me calm her down. I do not want her to go telling everyone the story I just told now. *(Rushes out too)*

Mnkong: *(Hands over his head)* This is corruption of innocence. The same Inspector who a year ago enjoined us to guard our moral rectitude is now corrupting a teenager. If the government knows that it is keeping groundnuts in a rat's hole, it will sack all the corrupt Inspectors *(He goes out and Yune enters, followed by Noyen)*.

Noyen: Yune hear me out. You are my friend.

Yune: Noyen, I hate you because you are too foolish. This is an opportunity for you to help reduce your mother's burden and improve her condition of living and you want to let it go just because of what Mnkong feels? Do not be worried about been caught because it will never happen. I have been having an affair with the Inspector of Health for two years now.

Noyen: *(Surprised)* You mean you started dating men when you were just in form two?

Yune: What is wrong about that? No one has ever suspected.

Noyen: *(Contemplatively)* I love my Mum. I will not do anything that displeases her. She will die if she thinks of…

Yune: Your mother's greatest wish is to see you up there, a woman of substance, dating the Inspector can take you there and besides you can always tell her that you are in school.

Noyen: Me! Deceive my mother?

Yune: I do that often. Sometimes, I even go on a day's filed trip.

Noyen: Your Mum is always busy on her farm or selling in the market. Besides you people are so many and so your absence may not even be noticed; mine does her work at home and I am her only child so we are closed. Our situations are not similar.

Yune: I will assist you.

Noyen: How?

Yune: Leave that for me to worry about. I am a guru in matters of the heart. I do not date only the Inspector of Health; I have Chung our classmate, my babe who is always there for me.

Noyen: (*Surprised*) you and Chung are a couple yet no one suspects? What if I get pregnant or I am infected? Do not forget Aids is real.

Yune: The Inspector is married and like every married man he will be prudent. He will do everything to protect himself and his family, so you have nothing to fear. It is good to deal with married men. With them you do not strain and the cash flows.

Noyen: How do you manage Chung?

Yune: You know his father is just a catechist. I use the cash I get from the Inspector to assist him in school so my word is law to him. He has never gotten to my Jerusalem or the one thing needful. I am not a cheap girl.

Noyen: My mother will kill me.

Yune: She will never know. I will always call round to inform you about the classes, so your mother will never even suspect.

Noyen: You talk as if I have accepted your advice.

Yune: You better accept because the Inspector's request is abundant grace from God.

Noyen: I will think about it.

Yune: Be fast because time is not on your side. (Pointing to Chung who is coming towards them) See who is coming! My Rose. We want to explore the new hot spot in Din. Often we go out of this village to prevent tongues from wagging and besides we do not want to be expelled from the lone school in our village.

Noyen: Let me go. I have a lot of catching up to do in school. (*She leaves while Yune moves towards Chung. Light fades out*)

Act II

Scene I

Noyen's home several months after. Noyen is now very sophisticated and arrogant)

Noyen: *(Care free)* Mama, We have a night class today.

Mother: *(Expressing doubt)* Night class, in this terse political atmosphere? These evening classes are now a thorn in my flesh. When will the class end?

Noyen: The teacher did not specify.

Mother: *(Sadly)* Noyen, is that the attire for a class? *(she leaves without responding)*

Mother: *(Runs after her)* what is happening to you my daughter? I have been quiet because I did not want to make the situation worse, but now I think it is worst. *(Angrily)* Go, but know that as you make your bed so shall you lie on it. *(She sits for a while with her hand on her chin, contemplates for a while then gathers items for a sacrifice: a keng life plant, some salt, a calabash of water and some cam wood).*

Mother: *(Slowly)* My ancestors: Tata, Father of the children Bih Maih, Nene Mom, Menkan, Mothers of our family If Noyen goes astray people will say you have not done your duty.

My hands are clean (*she drinks some of the water from the calabash and washes her face, pours some cam wood around the room and with the keng plant sprinkle some water on the four corners of the room*) Her fall is that of the family. My mothers and my fathers, guard Noyen and guide this generation. (*Sprinkling salt and robbing oil at the door post*) Let this salt neutralize every evil that will accompany her back to this house and let the oil sooths her wounds. Mnkong Moteh, protect her. (*She gathers her things and goes out*)

Scene II

(*At a road junction; the Inspector, dressed like a youth arrives joyously and waits for a while before Noyen arrives. She is gorgeously dressed. He hurries up to her, embraces her and admires her dress*).

Inspector Jerome: (*Caressing her*) You are alluring my baby. You are my Nebotiti. Where do you want us to go tonight?

Noyen: (*Smiling childishly*) Take me to town, specifically to the beach.

Inspector Jerome: (*Aside*) if she knows that my wife and her club members are at the beach tonight she will not ask that we go there. (*Back to her*) It will be too cold at the beach and you have not put on the attire for the beach.

Noyen: Then let's go to the botanic garden.

Inspector Jerome: The botanic garden! That is a place for poor people. Let's go to a hot spot, to any of those sophisticated night clubs where you will see girls of your age and know how beautiful you are.

Noyen: *(Still excited)* Okay, let's go anywhere; any place will be okay so long as I am with you.

Inspector Jerome: *(Taking her hand. Let us go my babey. Light goes out pop music and dancing are heard backstage for a period after which the Inspector and Noyen re-enter the stage that is now arranged as a bar. The Inspector looks exhausted but Noyen is excited)*

Noyen: *(dancing)* Sir, We should have stay at the hot spot a bit longer. All the recent hits were played (she dances more) The music was great.

Inspector Jerome: Do not call me Sir. Call me baby. *(Arranges her dress and sits her on one of the seats).* Baby, I hope I impressed you with the dance?

Noyen: Honey, you were wonderful and so full of life.

Inspector Jerome: What brand of drink will you take? I hope you will have some baby sham'. It is a classy gin. That hot spot was really hot and noisy. Here it is calmer and good for us to share our love. *(He kisses her hand)*

Noyen: I prefer a soft drink.

Inspector Jerome: *(adorably)* A soft drink will be ok but baby, you are not a child. Take the gin. It will make you sexy for me.

Noyen: You just called me baby and soft drinks are for babies.

Inspector Jerome: Noyen, I love your intelligence, I adore intelligent women. When I was in college I used to change girlfriends every week. I could risk having dull children.

Noyen: It is fun to be with you. Order the drinks so that we do not spend too much time here *(he calls the vendor who brings the drinks and Noyen serves them)*.

Inspector Jerome: *(Caressing her)* you are my baby.

Noyen: My Mum calls me baby, but I often tell her that I am now a grown up. My mum is so protective and I know she will die of worrying if I do not go home before midnight. *(contemplatively)* I have caused her so much pain since I started seeing you; *(looks at her watch)* I think I should be going home in an hour.

Inspector Jerome: *(Surprised)* You are returning? I thought we will spend the night in my hotel.

Noyen: We will do that some other time. I deceived my Mum and I know she is very worried.

Inspector Jerome: *(Taking her hand)* Forget about the old woman. When would you want us to get marry?

Noyen: *(Thoughtfully)* I cannot forget her. She loves and cares for me. She works tirelessly to pay for my education.

Inspector Jerome: *(Disappointed)* Okay, finish your drink and I will take you home. When will I be opportune to be in your angelic presence again?

Noyen: My exams begin in a fortnight so....

Inspector Jerome: *(Cuts in sarcastically)* Exams; you mean you will be reading 24houres?

Noyen: No, not that. I mean I will have little time to spare.

Inspector Jerome: *(Irritated)* Little time to spare. It seems you do not know how I enjoy your company or how much I long for the day you will be completely mine.

Noyen: *(happy)* Ok, I will create sometime for you on Friday night.

Inspector Jerome: *(Imposing)* You will spend that night with me on Friday. *(Noyen tries to argue but he kisses her, takes her hand and leads her out).* Let's go. It is nice that we return before midnight because highway robbers and occultists are on the increase.

Scene III

(In a classroom at school, a few days to exams. Nene is reading.)

Noyen: (Enters, *looking tire*) Good morning Nene.

Nene: Good morning Noyen. You have been as scarce as dog's tears. I was in your house on Friday and Sunday and your mum told me you were in school. I could not meet you in school because my parents do not allow me to go out at night. Here is a question I wanted you to assist me with *(Noyen sits down and studies the question)*. To tell you the truth Nene, this problem is above me. I have done very little work in preparation for this exam. If I don't sit up, I may not even pass the exam.

Nene: *(Worried)* what? What is the problem Noyen? Why have you not been studying? *(holding Noyen's hand and speaking slowly)* Noyen is everything alright?

Noyen: All is well Nene. I guess I'm just a bit distracted.

Nene: *(Concerned)* You Noyen, distracted? Is there something you are hiding from us? If Yune says she is distracted I will easily believe her, not you Noyen. Mnkong and Buji asked after you. They say you have not been regular in their study group. You refused to study with us saying we are lazy. Have the boys become lazy too? *(Pauses)* Noyen, I hope Yune is not leading you astray?

Noyen: Do not worry. I have a few problems but I am sorting things out. *(Nchioh comes in)*

Nchioh: Good morning Noyen. Have you seen the principal?

Noyen: What for?

Nene: There is a notice on the board stating that the principal wishes to see you.

Noyen: Me? I hope there is no problem. I hope I am not in trouble.

Nene: Please see the principal and find out *(Looks at her watch)*. I almost forgot that our study group meets at 10a.m. I will come to your house later. *(She goes out)*

Nchioh: Let me go with you Nene. I hope your group mates will allow me to join the group today. I have the feeling that the question you have will be repeated in this exam. Noyen I will see you in the evening.

Noyen: *(Alone and worried)* Am I alright? I am loosing focus. I sleep so much and I easily get tired. Let me see the principal before he leaves. *(She moves to the other part of the stage, the principal's office, knocks at the door and goes in)*

Noyen: Good morning sir.

Principal: Good morning my child *(continues to write)* sit down. *(Writes for a while)* how are you?

Noyen: I am fine sir. Thank you.

Principal: *(Stares at her)* Noyen, some years ago you were the jewel of this institution. You were the student that all the members of staff would proudly identify with, but it seems things have changed. For three months now I have heard rumour of your affair with the Inspector of Education. I did not believe the rumours because I assumed you are a decent girl whose only concern is to acquire education. However, four days ago I got rumour that you are pregnant so I have called you to get the truth from the horse's mouth. Is it true that you have an affair with the Inspector?

Noyen: *(Head down and fidgeting with her fingers)* Yes sir.

Principal: *(Surprised)* Is it true that you are pregnant?

Noyen: I do not know sir.

Principal: *(Sits Pitifully with his hands on his head for a while then says)* Oh, this is corruption of innocence. *(Emphatically)* Noyen, you know the school regulations. You will lose your place here if the pregnancy test is positive. Let's go to the district health post. *(They go out and shortly after, Noyen re-enters reading a letter and commenting)*

Noyen: *(Amazed and sad)* Oh God! This is not possible *(pauses)* but he is the only man I have ever had an affair with. *(annoyed)* He roped me of my virtues then calls me a whore? *(Continues to read and says in a resign manner)* Well, as he rightly states, the law is for them and if I try to seek justice, what he calls 'soil his reputation' he will as he promises, gives me hell here on earth. *(She looks at the letter for a while)*. Oh we of the unfortunate generation *(she collapses and Light fades out)*.

Scene IV

(In Noyen's home, two years after her expulsion from Kamsi Comprehensive College. She and her mother are doing needle work and discussing)

Mother: My daughter, I have enrolled you in Mr. Lobte's school. I hope you will not disappoint me again.

Noyen: *(Excited, throws down her work, kneels and takes her mother's hand)* Oh mother, I do not know how to thank you. I have learnt my lesson the hard way. I was misguided but I have realized that hard work and resistance to male exploitation is the god of women and I am going to worship that god. I will never fail you again. Thank you so much Mama and thank God that the anger of a mother does not last forever.

Mother: *(Happily)* A child is a good thing. I prayed for a child and I was elated when you came, but your situation was different. You wept when your baby came. You were a victim of men's cruelty. I wanted to give you the best and I still will.

Noyen: Mother, thank you so much for your love.

Mother: Go and look for Mesah while I prepare dinner *(They go out)*.

Scene V

In the Inspector's office, Inspector Caleb, a man of integrity has replaced Inspector Jerome. The Inspector is writing)

Mr. Kamsi: *(A handsome and elegantly dressed elite knocks and enters)* Good morning sir.

Inspector *Caleb*: *(Stops writing)* Good morning Mr. Kamsi, sit down. What brings you to my office so early in the morning? *(Mr. Kamsi gives him a letter which he reads and his countenance changes, then emphatically and angrily)* Why do you want Mr. Lobte's school to be closed down? *(Confused)* I thought the high level of illiteracy in this village is due to lack of educational Institutions. Mr. Lobte's efforts should be encouraged, not thwarted.

Mr. Kamsi: *(Boldly)* You are mistaking sir; illiteracy in my village is high because parents do not send children to school. They marry too many wives and produce many children who end up as prostitutes and arm robbers. *(Emphatically)* Can you imagine Inspector, the fee in my school is just thirty thousand minas yet they do not enrol their children.

Inspector Caleb: Mr. Lobte offers Vocational Education and the fee is just twenty thousand Minas; don't you think this will encourage some poor parents to send children to school?

Mr. Kamsi. That is why I am here. It worries me.

Inspector Caleb: *(Surprised)* Instead?

Mr. Kamsi: My school used to be crowded but the number of students has reduced greatly and this means reduction in profit.

Inspector Caleb: *(scornfully)* profit. Mr. Kamsi, when one invests in his village his interest in the development of the village should take precedence over his selfish interest *(he opens his drawer brings out a letter and places on the table).* This is a protest letter written by the poisant of your village against the hospital the government intended to construct next year. Do you know what they say?

Mr. Kamsi: *(Just smiles)*

Inspector Caleb: They say they do not want the hospital now because it will increase the popularity of the Lumeto party. Is the hospital for the people or a party? Will the poisants not be attended to at the hospital? I do not understand your people.

Mr. Kamsi: Mr. Inspector, you are an Administrator and so a member of the Lumeto party. I will confide in you. That letter was written by us, member of the Lumeto party so as to discredit the poisants. Do not delay the letter, send it immediately to hierarchy.

Inspector Caleb: *(Angry)* Members of the Lumeto party wrote this letter? You are willing to sacrifice the development of your village just to discredit the poisant? I am an Administrator and a politician, but I believe in

31

communal interest first. *(Mr. Kamsi gives him another envelope. He opens it sees the money in it).*

Inspector Caleb: *(Returns the envelope to Kamsi and peaks slowly and lovingly)* Mr. Kamsi, I am a Rotarian. Rotarians are guided by the four way test in what they think do and say. The four way test).

i)   Is it the truth?
ii)   Is it fair to all concerned?
iii)   Will it builds good will and better friendship?
iv)   Will it be beneficial to all concerned?

What you expect me to do is a difficult task because it violates the four way test. It is not fair and beneficial to all concerned nor does it build good will and better friendship.

Mr. Kamsi: *(Excited).* It is nice to hear that you are a Rotarian. I am a Rotarian too and the four way test is even the anthem of my college. My school has benefited a lot from Rotary's vocational services. This envelope is just a token of my appreciation for your honesty and hard work.

Inspector Caleb: *(Ignores him and continues to write)* you need to review your understanding of the principle of Rotary International. *(writes for a while then stops suddenly and says angrily)* Mr. Kamsi, if you do not mind, I have a few things to attend to. *(Kamsi leaves disappointed).*

Kamsi: *(Outside the Inspector's office boastfully)* I will go to hierarchy. Mr. Rotarian will feel so little when Lobte's school is closed down. He missed an opportunity to grab cool cash. *(Angry)* Who does he think he is? Where does he think he is, in Acirema? Even Trump evaded taxes. *(Calms down)* if I had such an opportunity I will send my family on a luxury holiday abroad. Mr. Rotarian is a fool, a hypocrite who claims to love our village more than we do. He will suffer for his mistakes *(Leaves the state and light fades out)*

Scene VI

In Noyen's home, Noyen's mother is selecting vegetable

Noyen: *(Rushes in dejected)* Mother! Mother, have you heard? Have you heard the bad news?

Mother: *(Getting up)* What bad news?

Noyen: Our school has been shut down.

Mother: *(Unconcerned)* shut down? Why? *(Pauses and then emphatically and confidently)* Do not despair. That school will never be closed down, not even by Mr. Lobte its owner. When we the Febien of this village heard it rumoured that some elites wanted the school closed down, we went into covenants about the school. I will see Mr. Lobte and if what you say is true, the women of this village will make a declaration. *(Angrily)*Enough is enough. We must take the destiny of our children into our hands. *(Calmly)* Be at peace my daughter. (She leaves).

Noyen: (*Talks to herself while selecting the vegetable her mother left*) How can I be at peace when my world is about to crumble again? Whatever happens, I will continue my education, even if it means going out of this village. I have known that when there is the will, there is always a way. I have the will so there must be a way. (*she selects the vegetables for while then hears the horn of Febien summoning women for their meeting*) The horn of Febien? Our mothers have taken over power. Every woman must support them. Let me go and support them. (*she leaves*)

Scene VII

The Febien meeting, the atmosphere is sombre.

Leader: My fellow women, you all know why we are here today. A few months ago, we heard it rumoured that Mr. Kamsi wanted Mr. Lobte's school, the school that has provided the opportunity for many poor women to send their children to school closed down. The rumour is now a reality. The school has been closed down and our men seem powerless or, let me say they do not care since they do not send children to school. We are the ones who pay for our children's education and the ones who are blamed when children go astray, so we are the ones to act. Mr. Kamsi has declared war on the women and no man fights with a woman and no win. (*Emphatically*) Women, what should we do since our lions are now sheep? I want three suggestions.

Noh Yune: *(Angry)* We should perform our rituals and visit Mr. Kamsi's school. We will close down that school. He cannot dare the women.

Noh Mom: We have the power to do so, but that will be contrary to our vision for this village. We need more schools so we will not close down any. We want a thousand flowers to blossom. We have issues with Mr. Kamsi, not with his school.

Noh Noyen: I agree with Noh Mom. I suggest the Febien takes a keng, the peace plant to Mr. Kamsi and implores him to do whatever he did to have the school closed down so that the school be reopened. If we close down Kamsi's school we are making our situation more difficult. What happens to our children in that school? What we want is development. I suggest our sister Noh Maih and a few others be given that assignment.

Noh Nchioh: What if he rejects our plea?

Leader: I think Noh Noyen's suggestion is good. Remember we are good wives and must respect our husbands and Mr. Kamsi is one of them. I also strongly believe that Mr. Kamsi will not turn down our plea. He will be on his heels to have the decree closing the school revoked because he is not a stranger in this village. He knows that not even the Fon, nor can the Kwifon battle with the Febien and succeed. *(Pauses and then emphatically and slowly)* if per chance he ignores our plea then we will meet again to do what Febien does in situations like this. Meanwhile Mr. Lobte's school remains open. Our children will continue to go to school. Whosoever attempts to stop them will receive the wrath of Febien.

Noh Yune: It is unfortunate that Mr. Kamsi who should be fighting for the development of this village does the contrary. Taking a keng to him is not enough. We should expect more from Mr. Kamsi. We should compel him to establish a high school in his college.

All: (*Joyously*) That is a perfect idea.

Leader: Noh Maih, Noh Noyen and Noh Yune will come to my house at midnight so that we perform the ritual to empower them for the assignment. I want to remind members that Febien discussions are sacred and secret, so be on the guard. The horn of Febien will summon you again if there is need (*They exit in a solemn manner*)

Act III

Scene I

In Nchioh's supermarket, Mnkong enters and is greeted by Nchioh

Nchioh: Mnkong, Welcome to my humble shop.

Mnkong: You call this humble? This is a supermarket.

Nchioh: Just to make ends meet (*showing him a sit*) sit down let me offer you a drink.

Mnkong: (*Sits down and surveys the place*) Wao! This is wonderful.

Nchioh: (*Smiling*) And you Mnkong, what have you been up to? This is your first visit to the village since we graduated. I guess you are working in one of those big offices in Dom, or have you fallen Bush?

Mnkong: No. (*Pauses*) I live with my uncle. Since I left the university I have been running a barbing saloon, but that is just for now; I intend to continue my studies. I have applied for post graduate studies.

Nchioh: (*Laughing*) Bookworm. A first degree is not enough for you? What I need now is a job. I am tired of writing applications and attending interviews in vain.

Mnkong: Does it mean you have no plans to continue with your studies?

Nchioh: What for? Look at what I do after earning a degree in engineering. Where is the incentive for one to pursue further studies?

Mnkong: *(Unaffected)* the situation in which we are is temporary. I believe things will change.

Nchioh: There will be a change if we stop being who we are, selfish nepotic and tribalistic. I lack a job not because there are no jobs, but because someone is guarding the job for his daughter, niece, nephew, brother or cousin who is yet to enrol in engineering or because I am the enemy in the house.

Mnkong: Do not cloud your vision with all the negativities in Kala. We are in the global village and no one can stop us. *(Proudly)* we are hardworking and honest so the sky is our limit. Prepare to go for your MA.

Nchioh: Illusion.

Mnkong: *(Changing the topic)* I heard Kamsi's College had 100% in the advanced level.

Nchioh: Yes, and Noyen had five paper with 22 points.

Mnkong: Noyen is wonderful. She would have been a graduate if she had not been deceived by that wicked Inspector and Yune.

Nchioh: Yune, I heard she is at Dom. Have you met her?

Mnkong: She is one of the big ladies in Dom. She rides luxurious cars and dresses ostentatiously. I hear she is married to a rich businessman from Arenia.

Nchioh: Give me her contact address. I buy most of the provisions in my shop from Dom. I will like to call on her for old time sake.

Mnkong: I have just her phone number let me look for it *(He writes it on a paper and gives to her)* let me go and congratulate Noyen. I hope she enrols in the University.

Nchioh: Do you doubt that? For her the sky is her limit. Let me accompany you, I have not yet congratulated her *(to her sales girl)* Joy take care of the shop *(they leave)*

Scene II

In Nchioh's house three years later; Nchioh is sitting on a chair close to her television set and is examining her certificate and graduation pictures. Noyen knocks and is invited in.

Noyen: Good day Nchioh. I went to your supermarket and you were not in so I decided to check on you at home.

Nchioh: (Still examining the pictures) My sister, I decided to stay at home today. Sometimes I feel really bitter.

Noyen: *(Surprise)* Bitter? Why? You have so many things to be thankful for. *(Playfully)*You are not second hand as they

39

say I am (*smiling to cheer her up*). You have your degree, a good restaurant and a supermarket. I am still struggling to get a degree.

Nchioh: (*Cuts in angrily, throwing the pictures at Noyen*) Look at these pictures, the euphoria in them. (*Giving Noyen her certificate*)Take this paper and look at it. Three years after graduation I am still jobless. The only job I can get is teaching which I hate so much. I did civil engineering hoping to work with one of the oil or road construction companies; but since I am not a frog and I am neither the daughter of a parliamentarian nor that of a minister, my dreams cannot be achieved.

Noyen: Nchioh, you surprise me. I thought you were happy with what you are doing. Besides the fact that you are making much money, you are serving humanity, and I think that is the whole essence of education. There is profit in service.

Nchioh: That is not the problem. My supermarket and restaurant are the best in this village. I make much money and I love the service I render to mankind, but do I need a degree in engineering to run a supermarket? What is the difference between Yune and me? I need to put into practice the knowledge I acquired in school. That is the only way I can be fulfilled.

Noyen: You wish to be like me? Like Yune? Like Mnkong? Like Buji? Like Chung?

Nchioh: Why not? *(Pauses)* Sometimes I envy all of you. Look at me, jobless, husbandless and childless *(pauses)*... All the lesses.

Noyen: Moneyless and homeless? *(Irritated)* What do you want and who prevents you from getting it? For how long have you been bitter? *(Lovingly)* My mother has no husband and no job, yet she works every minute of the day and is always happy. I have just graduated, five years after my classmates. I am still jobless; I am not even thinking of a husband but I am happy. Mnkong who is abroad may not be as comfortable as we think. You cannot know where a shoe pinches until you wear it. If you so much despise what you do then why have you been in this village all these years? You know an oil company job will not be gotten in this village. Keep moving while weeping *(pauses)*. Nchioh, why have you changed? You love to be like Yune?

Nchioh: Why not? Yune dropped out of school in form four. She does not even have the ordinary level, but she is married, she drives big cars and you need to see her beautiful children. Her house is classic. Why should I not envy her?

Noyen: I ran into Yune two weeks ago and she took me home, gave me expensive wine, showed me round her classy home and introduced me to her beautiful children. You know what?

Nchioh: What?

Noyen: She confided in me and I love her for her honesty. She says the wealth she enjoys only bring out her hollowness. She was envious of me. She has come to know that education empowers. She desires to go back to school but her rich husband does not permit her. I spoke with her husband and he agreed to let her attend an evening school. You are envious of someone who despises her situation. Yune is just lucky, marriage is luck. Women mean different things to men. To men like Jeff, Yune's husband woman is a goddess that must be adored. These type of men love and provide for every need of their wives. Some men see women as food; those suck their wives of every material and spiritual gift. If a woman married to this type does not realize who her man is on time, she drifts into nothingness, becomes disillusioned and could go crazy or die. Others see women as partners and help mates. Women married to such men are fulfilled and together they blossom. Not everyone is lucky in marriage.

Nchioh: *(Looks at the wall clock and exclaims)* My God! I am almost late for fellowship. *(Putting on her shoes and gathering her things)* Noyen, can you accompany me to church?

Noyen: I will because my mother will cook today but I hope we will not stay there till late?

Nchioh: No. You will be so engrossed that you will not even notice the time. Let us go *(as they leave they meet Maggie, Nchioh's mother at the entrance).*

Noyen: Mummy welcome.

Nchioh: *(Cuts in)* Mummy, we are almost late for fellowship.

Maggie: You still talk of fellowship? I thought we settled this matter yesterday.

Nchioh: *(Irritated)* Mum, I gave my life to Christ just two weeks ago so I need to attend these fellowships to grow in the Lord.

Maggie: Every day? *(Pauses)* My daughter, I am not against God; what I fear is this fanaticism. It will take you nowhere. It will kill your reasoning and make your situation worse. There are many examples to cite.

Nchioh: On the contrary Mama, I find peace when I sing, dance and cry especially when I am under the power of the Holy Spirit.

Noyen: What your mama is saying is right Nchioh. Your feeling of peace is temporary and illusive. I attended one of these fellowships when I visited my aunt in Airegin. They fellowshipped from Monday to Sunday; pastors want to keep the euphoria that all is well, so they intoxicate the Christians daily. Each day they talk of prosperity and this makes those who feel they have not arrived envious and bitter.

Maggie: Noyen, talk to your friend. She has become so bitter lately. Let me go, I am also late for our Febien meeting. I do not want to pay a fine *(She leaves)*

Nchioh: *(Happy)* Let us go. I am really late. *(They leave)*

Scene III

At the church Noyen and Nchioh enter, sit and start praying; others who look dejected and poorly dressed join them, the Pastor and his group enter. They are healthy and ostentatiously dressed. All others stand and cheer as they enter)

Pastor: Prai…….se the Lord.

Members: Al le lu yah!

Pastor: The Lord is good.

Members: All the time.

Pastor: You are very welcome to our fellowship of today. Turn to your neighbour and say my miracle is around *(they do)*. Tell your neighbour that you will not let God go until He blesses you *(they do) (To sister Blessing)* Sister Blessing, lead us in praise and worship. You know what praises do to God. *(dramatizing)* when we praise God, He gets up and begins to shower us with blessings *(sister Blessing leads the congregation in praise worship for a while. People dance, shout, sleep on the ground, cry, etc.)*

Pastor: Clap for Jesus *(they clap)*. Our God is good.

Members: All the time.
Pastor: And all the time.

Members: The Lord is good.

Pastor: Let us pray. Our alpha and omega, we thank you for a day like this. Bless especially those that are in our church today for the first time. Teach them to know that whatsoever we sow, that we shall reap. Lay not your treasures here on earth. You are the fortunate few who have their names in the book of life. I will work miracles for you. The crippled walk, the blind see, thousands of sick people are healed. The spirit of the Lord is on me. Two months ago I was in Mboh and cancer was cured. Praise the Lord.

Members: Hallelujah!

Pastor: When I was in Kevu a year ago, a woman that had been childless for twelve years conceived and a man who was about to be buried was brought back to life. There were many testimonies. Is the lord not wonderful?

Members: Applause.

Pastor: He does these things only to those who have sown seeds of faith. What do we have here in our village? (*Emphatically*) Mothers who have abandoned the church for the Febien. Last week I went to Ibal where our mothers were having their Febien meeting. I had hoped to talk some sense into them. When they saw me they started singing insulting songs. They say the church is the cause of the misery in the land (*demonstrating*) I brought out the cross of our Lord and said; 'This is the way, the truth and the life. Everyone

45

was quite. The Holy Spirit was in control (*shouts of joy from the congregation*) then one of the women walked up to me and took the cross. I was dumbfounded. Holding up the cross she said 'this is the symbol of exploitation, the symbol of disunity and the symbol of impending doom in our society'. She threw the cross into the pot of sacrifice and I just left because the battle is the Lord's. I visited our honourable parliamentarian last night and met this eldest son in pain. He said he had been visited by the Febien which accused him of corruption and injustice. He feels the ritual they performed is the cause of his son's illness. His son died this morning and that is why he is not in church. His son, John was a good and devoted Christian. He paid all his church dues and even donated a million for the pastor's car. He is surely in heaven where he laid his treasures. We are in perilous times so no one should lay his treasures here on earth (*To sister Tarn*) Sister Tarn, lead us in praises while we sow our seeds of faith (*Baskets are brought out. A variety of dance styles are seen as the people offer their gifts. The pastor gives nothing. He watches them in admiration. This last for about five minutes*)

Pastor: (*Hilariously*) The lord is good.

Members: All the time.

Pastor: (*Emphatically*) And all the time.

Members: The lord is good.

Pastor: (*slowly*) Thank you for sowing. Now that you have sown, expect a bounteous harvest because after sowing is harvesting. My Jesus will multiply whatsoever you have given today a thousand times. Lift up your hands so that I pray for you. (*They lift up their hands while he prays*) May God bless and keep you.

Members: Amen.

Pastor: May your cup run over and may His light shine on you throughout your life.

Members: Amen.

Pastor: May you never stop giving because it is better to give than to receive.

Members: Amen.

Pastor: Yes! It is better to give than to receive. It is by giving that this Ministry, All Saints Ministry has grown. Prior to the birth of our Ministry, the devil had caged me. I spent five years and above three million in SAMS for a degree in Marine technology but had no degree. We did not even take the final exam; it was one story after another. I was frustrated and my parents disappointed. My loving God gave me a job as a clerk in one of our government institutions. My salary of 20.000 Minas was the seed I sown. I was not Ananias and Sapphire. For a year I did not use even a mina of my salary, I gave God all and he made me what I am today. There is no seed that is too big or too small. What matters is where you give and whether you have given all. This Ministry offers you an opportunity for double your blessings.

Members: Aaaaaaaaaaaaaaaaaaaaaamen

Pastor: (*Jumping from one part of the stage to another*) sowing time!

Members: (*Shouting*) Blessing time.

Noyen: (*Aside*) Sowing time again? This pastor wants to milk his congregation dry.

Pastor: Yes blessing time. Ushers bring out the baskets. The lord is going to meet some one's need today. Miracles are about to happen but you must do your part. The spirit of God is here. sheeeeeeeeeeeeeeeee. Quiet! (*After a few seconds*) A modern house! You desire a modern house, sow a seed (*people rushed to the alter to sow seeds*) someone is about to get a life partner. Sow your seed and tell God the type of life partner you want. (*Youths rush to the alter*) Your Samuel is on the way.

Members: Aaaaaaaaaaaaaaaamen

Pastor: You have been called barren, come out and sow a seed for your Samuel (*a multitude of women rush out*). You deserve a better car, sister saw a seed. (*a multitude rush out*) I see someone in a plane, has your visa been delayed, sow a seed. (*sowing of seed goes on goes on for five minutes*). Now that we have sown our seeds let us all stand and drive the devil. (*They stand, the pastor sings the solo and they sing the chorus, they dance as if the stronger the dance the faster the devil will leave and their situations will become better)*

Pastor: Poverty

Members: Manifest and go

Pastor: Sickness

Members: Manifest and go

Pastor: Hatred

Members: Manifest and go

Pastor: Suffering

Members: Manifest and go. *(Singing and dancing last for two minutes, some members fall to the ground)*

Pastor: Prai...................se the Lord!

Members: Aaaaaaaaaaaaaaaaaaaaaaleluya!

Pastor: We have come to the end of today's service. Those who are attending the church for the first time should wait. We want to know you more so as to be able to solve your problems *(congregation begins to disperse)*.

Nchioh: Noyen, you have to wait and see the pastor.

Noyen: (*Sarcastic*) What for?

Nchioh: This is your first time of attending.

Noyen: (*disdainful*) I do not want to become a member of your church, your pastor tells so many lies.

Nchioh: (*Getting angry*) Lies? Why do you say so? He is a powerful man of God.

Noyen: (*In a mockery*) Powerful man of God. His lie about the meeting with the Febien, our mothers' cult; my mother is the leader of febien, if such a thing happened she would have told me. He lied about miracles he performed but did not even notice the blind man on the first bench and what about the cripple in the choir? Does he not deserve a miracle?

Nchioh: The minds of people who are not born again are so critical. God's ways are not like ours. Noyen, be careful how you talk about the things of God. Let us go. I am connected. I do not want to get involve in earthly discussions. This world is not any home.

Noyen: (Resigned) Nchioh, you have always been a practical person so I am really surprised at your naivety. Remember those days when we use to say that hard work is the God of women. I hope you will soon stop deceiving yourself. That man is just exploiting his members. Let us go, my mother should be worried since I did not tell her that I will be late.

Nchioh: God is on the throne.

Noyen: Nchioh, why don't you further your studies? I will advise again 'while waiting keep moving'. I applied for postgraduate studies in Arenia. Mnkong told me the admission list is usually published in April so it is not late for you to apply. Since you have not gotten a job with a Degree, go for a Master. It will place you a step ahead.

Nchioh: Noyen, as I told you before, these days I need to pray before I take any decision. I need to be sure that whatever I do is God's will.

Noyen: Then start praying now and listen not only to the voice of fanaticism but to that of reason. *(They go out)*

Scene IV

At Noyen's home, she and her mother are sitting on the veranda and she is doing her mother's hair. Yaya, a former school mate comes in with a letter for Noyen.

Yaya: Good day mama.

Mother: Welcome my daughter.

Yaya: Hi Noyen.
Noyen: Hi Yaya *(Going to get a sit for her)* let me get a chair for you.

Yaya: No, thanks. I just came to give your mail. I will not stay for long. (*she gives her the letter*)

Noyen: Thank you (*turning to her mother*) Mama, just a minute, let me see off Yaya. (*they leave and she returns a few seconds after. She opens the letter and after reading for a while she exclaims*) Mama! God has done it again!

Mother: (*Excited*) What is it my daughter?

Noyen: Mnkong says I have been granted admission for postgraduate studies in Arenia.

Mother: (*Embraces her daughter and sings 'I will sing hallelujah song. (she dances for a while)* Noyen, this is the best news you have given me since you graduated. I was getting bored of your presence in this house.

Noyen: (*Embracing her Mom and Joking*) Mama you are lying. I know you will miss me a lot; especially as I will be taking my little girl with me.

Mother: (*Smiling*) Do not deceive yourself, you have no little girl in this house; remember she calls me mum, and you sister.

Noyen: (*Smiling*) I will miss both of you a lot.

Mother: When are schools expected to begin?
Noyen: In a month's time, (*Very excited*) that is what Mnkong says. Let me go and share the good news with Nchioh and the others

Mother: Please finish plaiting my hair.

Noyen: *(Smiling)* Mum, I will do that when I return. *(she leaves)*

Mother: (*A monologue*) I doubt if my savings will be enough to finance her studies in Arenia. I will see her uncle and ask for help. *(pauses)* I doubt if he will assist. He is amongst those who believe that a woman's place is in the kitchen. *(a short silence)*I know that where there is the will there is a way. I will see Mr. Lobte, I believe he will lend me some money. (*she leaves*)

Act IV

Scene I

In Arenia at the school of postgraduates studies

Noyen: *(knocks and goes in)* Good morning sir.

Secretary: Good morning. Can I help you?

Noyen: I am one of the newly admitted postgraduate students. I wish to collect my admission letter.

Secretary: What is your name and what is the department into which you were admitted.

Noyen: My name is Nchindah Noyen. I was admitted into the Department of Law.

Secretary: *(He goes through the list for a while)* Sorry you were not offered admission.

Noyen: But, but, a friend of mine informed me that I was admitted. He said my supervisor is Professor Wekins.

Secretary: Give me a minute. Let me get the list of candidates rejected so that we can find out what the problem is in your case.

Noyen: Thank you sir.

Secretary: (*Returns shortly after with a buddle of files, sits and begins to go through them*). I have seen your name. From the records I have here, it is evident that the department recommended you for admission but the postgraduate school could not get either a translated version of your transcript or the evaluation system used by institutions in your country.

Noyen: We have an embassy here. I hope it will be of help.

Secretary: We contacted your embassy.

Noyen: What did they say?

Secretary: They said you were not qualified.

Noyen: Our ambassador said that? (*Lights out*)

Scene II

Flashback. An Admission Board Meeting in Arenia, the members are seated on a round table studying files for admission

Dean: Let us proceed because we have so many cases to examine. We examined the file of candidate no 14 before you went for the coffee break so the next candidate should be number 15. Over to you Mr. Nkem.

Mr. Nkem: The next candidate in the department of Law is Noyen Nchindah. She has been recommended by her department and her reference reports are excellent. Her performance is excellent because she has an overall average of 89 on 100. Every other thing on the transcript is in French. (*he tries to read out some of the French words but is unable*)

Dean: Mr. Lam, take the transcript to the French department for translation and interpretation. (*Mr. Lam goes out*)

Dr. Mais: The candidate has 89% so she is qualified because the PGS requirement stipulates that candidates with unclassified degrees are qualified if they have above 50%.

HOD/Law: Students from Kale are hard working. Those in our Faculty always top their classes.

Prof. Numso: That is true but it does not mean that every student who applied from Kale should be admitted.

Mr. Nkem: (*Returns with the transcript and sits down*) The sum of ten thousands pises is needed for the translation.

Dean: Go to the next case. We have done our best. We have already wasted so much time on this candidate.

HOD/Law: I plead that this student be offered admission. We had the same problems in our departmental admission board but we recommended her because her scores are excellent. She was the best amongst the applicants we had.

Mr. Nkem: I suggest we call the Kalean embassy.

All: That is a good suggestion.

Dean: Mr. Nkem: What is the number of the Kalean embassy?

Mr. Nkem: (*Looks into a directory and reads*) 43445823.

Dean: (*Dials the number and listen*)

Kalean Secretary: (*off stage*). This is the Kalean embassy. Can we help you?

Registrar: Could you link me to your Ambassador?

Kalean Secretary: (*off stage*). Okay, hold on sir. (*Still off stage, to the Ambassador*) Monsieur, c'est pour vous. Ça vient de l'université d'Arenia.

Ambassador: (*off stage*) Demand leur ce qu'ils veulent.

Kalean Secretary: (*off stage*) Hello sir! Can I help you?

Registrar: Thank you sir, one of your students applied for postgraduate studies in our university and we are having problems in evaluating the transcript. What we see on the transcript is 76 and très bien

Kalean Secretary: (*off stage*).Hold on for a minute sir (*to the Ambassador*). Ils dissent qu'un de nos étudiants a eu l'admission dans leur établissement et ils veulent savoir s'il est qualifié.

Ambassador: *(off stage and aside)* No, no, no, no. Les Olignas, il vient ici, avoir les diplôme et âpre ils rentrent au pays pour nos opposer

Kalean Secretary: *(off stage, back on phone)* The grade trebien does not qualify a Kalean for postgraduate's studies.

Dean: The student has 89%

Kalean Secretary: *(off stage. Cutting in emphatically)* Even if the student has 99% he or she is not qualify.

Dean: Thank you for your cooperation. *(to the other members)* You heard what the ambassador said. The student is not qualified for postgraduate studies. Let us move on. We have so many files to study.

Registrar: The next candidate is …

(Light fades out)

Scene III

In Mnkong's house in Arenia. Noyen knocks and enters.

Mnkong: How do you enjoy life here Noyen? I have been too busy preparing for my proposal defence that I have not had time to show you around the place.

Noyen: Everything is ok. Just that nothing has changed. The secretary at the PG School keeps giving me one appointment after another but nothing has changed.

Mnkong: I feel responsible for the situation in which you are now Noyen. I should have waited for the final admission list to be published before informing you. I do not know why your case is different because usually the admission commission just confirms the proposals of the departments.

Noyen: (*Light hearted*) My case is always different. Do not torture yourself. We have been childhood friends and you know that for me nothing good comes easy. Whatever the situation, I do not believe that God brought me from Kale to Arenia just to disappoint me.

Mnkong: Noyen, I envy your courage and your faith in God. Some other girl would have been lamenting and regretting, but you do not give up in times of difficulties.

Noyen: There is nothing to regret. The job I had at home could not even provide for my needs. Here I can do a lot of things to survive. I have sold all the backrests my mum and I made and I have sent a message asking her to send more. I have just one option which is to stay here and do whatever I need to do to succeed. Prof. Pal who bought a set of backrest, has promised to link me to his brother, a wholesaler of cloths. Besides the backrests, I will begin to sell cloth. I will leave no stone unturned.

Mnkong: Talking about turning stones, I think you should see the Head of your department tomorrow. He is fatherly and I believe when he sees you he will do everything to ensure that your journey here is not in vain.

Noyen: I will. The Registrar said our embassy was contacted and they said I was not qualified. I can't understand why our embassy should say that.

Mnkong: Fear.

Noyen: Fear of what?

Mnkong: An Oligna Lawyer. It is people like you that will begin to ask questions and asking for a redress of the situation in Kale.

Noyen: Then they should be ready to give up the ghost because there are a thousand Oligna lawyers in the making just here in Arenia not to think of those in other parts of the worlds *(standing)* let me leave so that you can continue to study. A sister invited me to her fellowship; since I have some time to spare I will attend.

Mnkong: Know that I am always here for you.

Noyen: Thank you.

Mnkong: You are welcome. *(They leave and shortly after the HOD enters and sits on a table on the other part of the stag. Noyen knocks and enters)*

Noyen: Good morning sir.

HOD: Good morning my daughter, sit down (*pauses*) Can I help you?

Noyen: I am Noyen Nchindah, one of the students from Kale who applied for the postgraduate admission in this department.

HOD: Welcome. You look as smart as I thought when I went through your application file. We recommended you for admission but your transcript was in French and we could not get it translated.

Noyen: Sir, I need your assistance. I left the job I had at home so I cannot even go back home.

HOD: Do not despair. I will recommend to the PG school that you be admitted with some remedial courses. I am aware that the Oglnas in Kale are discriminated against. We are your brothers so it is our duty to assist you. I love students from Kale because they are hard working. Start attending classes so that you will not be behind when the problem is resolved and you are admitted.

Noyen: (*kneeling down*) Thank you very much sir.

HOD: Get up my daughter all is well. (*she continuously thanks the Head as she leaves*) Let me go to the PG school now. This is a pride student who will take over from us. If we want to protect our profession we must hand our legacies to students like her. She will be my supervisee and we will co-author several intellectual discourses. (*He leaves*).

Scene IV

At Mnkong's flat.

Noyen: (*Rushes in without knocking and shouts*) Mnkong! Mnkong oh!

Mnkong: (*Running out of the kitchen*) Yes! What is the matter Noyen?

Noyen: A miracle has taken place. (*She started singing and dancing*)
'My God is alive 2x.
My Jesus is alive, the hope of my life.
I want you to know as I also know that my Jesus is alive.
Oh yes He is alive.
(*Joyously*) I am starting classes tomorrow.

Mnkong: Classes tomorrow, how?

Noyen: (*Excited*) I saw the Head of Department as you recommended. He is such a nice daddy. He suggested that I take some remedial courses along with the master's programme. He promised to sort out things at the postgraduate school and advised that I start attending classes tomorrow.

Mnkong: (*Embracing her happily*) I am so happy for you. Sit down. We have to celebrate. Let me get some wine.

Noyen: (*She sits down, Mnkong brings two glasses and a bottle of wine which he opens and serves*) I am so happy. This is America for me, my land of promise.

Mnkong: I am happy for you too. Let's toast.

Noyen: Let us toast for success in all we do, and for more kaleians to be admitted into this great university.

Mnkong: (*Cuts in jokingly*) And for marriage. Don't you think we need to settle down and start making tomorrow's generation?

Noyen: Count me out.

Mnkong: (*Still joking*) what if I proposed?

Noyen: (*Seriously*) Stop joking Mnkong, you are like a brother to me. (*pauses and changes the topic*) What do you think we can do to encourage more of our classmates to apply to study here?

Mnkong: (*Ignoring her question*) Just like, but not your brother

Noyen: Please! Stop. Stop imagining things that should not be. What do you think we can do to persuade Nchioh to apply to study here?

Mnkong: (*Giving up on the issue of Marriage*) Noyen, I was about to cook when you came, now that you are here I will assist you in the cooking. Let us go to the kitchen.

Noyen: (*Standing*) What should we cook? Ife sala? Ugbono? Fried rice? Ubaka or Achicha? I am so excited.

Mnkong: Me too! (*Taking her by the hand*) Let us cook some paye stuff and get some bear to celebrate the way we do at home. You know home is home. (*They leave as light fades*)

Scene V

At Mawes Banque Hall. Some Ex-students of Kamsi Comprehensive College are having a drink after celebrating the Silver jubilee of the college. Present are Professor Peter Mnkong now husband to, Justice Noyen Nchindah-Mnkong Dr. Engineer Nchioh, Rev Dr. Bishop Chung, pharmacist Yaya, Mrs Yune - Njoya and Nene who is a medical doctor in Acirema. Though twenty-five years have passed they still look young elegant and happy.

Prof. P. Mnkong: We need to do more for KCC our Alma matter. KCC was our saviour. The government in its desire to punish the poisant neglected the welfare of its citizens. We are what we are today thanks to the efforts of Mr Kamsi. I am the luckiest. I got not only education from KCC but my wife, my angel, my rose in winter, Justice Noyen.

Yune- Njoya: I remember how you were very protective of her back then. Noyen did you know he will be your husband?

Justice Noyen-Mnkong: No. If he had proposed to me back then we won't be married today.

Yune, Njoya: It is said that marriages are made in heaven. I have grown to know that life is not a game where the fastest and the swiftest win, but a gift from God and God is in control. *(Proudly)* Look at me, I am now a teacher, enrolled in a distant learning degree programme; did any of us know this will happen?

Dr. Engineer Nchioh: True my sister God controls life. I have learned that it is never too late to start all over. After ten years of stagnation and bitterness, I started all over and I have still achieved my dream.

Rev Dr. Chung: God's mercies are new every moment and no one can change His plans. Often I look back in anger at my school days. I imagine the souls I would have won for Christ and how much I would have done to prevent the fanaticism that has hijacked Christianity. Each time the Lord uses me to teach the Truth about Christianity I feel fulfilled and then I begin to think of the years wasted. The years I wasted in night clubs chasing shadows. What consoles me is the fact that we have no power of our own, on our own we can do nothing but we can do all things through Christ who strengthens us. The harvest is ready and everyone:

teachers Doctors Justices, lawyers and even children have to be part of the harvest.

Justice Noyen-Mnkong: We have so much to be thankful for. The Four Way Test, the Anthem of Kamsi CC has become my motto. In every court session I do not only emphasize on the truth but I ensure that it is fair to all concern, that it is beneficial to all concerned and that it will build goodwill and better friendship. When I handle a case even the convicted are pleased that justice is done.

Pharmacist Yaya: My sister we are thankful to know that we have a Justice like you. I have heard how the righteous shout for joy when they hear that you are the one to handle their case files and how the wicked tremble in fear knowing all their wicked plans will be unveil and justice will prevail.

Dr. Engineer Nchioh: The Lord is our strength. We have to be thankful for our mothers who never gave up on us and from whom we have learned to be good mothers. My father left for the coast when my mum was pregnant, his corpse was brought home when I was ten years old. Like many of the children in our village I did not know the love of a father.

Pharmacist Yaya: I had a father yet I have not had a father's love because it has always been my mum; from a childhood she has been my provided, protector and guard; that is why I find it difficult to say "The 'Our

Father'. It easier to say Our mother who are in Heaven because my mum has being my God.

All: *(Laughing)* That is funny Yaya.

Mrs. Yune – Njoya: My case was worse. I learned to be a good parent from lack of good parenting. My parents, great business people provided every material thing I needed but not loved. I sought for love in vain from my numerous boyfriends and then I came to understand that children need love more than material things. I am always there for my children, each day I kiss them and tell them how much I love them. This has really paid up. My daughter who will be graduating from our lone University in six weeks is still a virgin while I lost my virginity just in form one. You are all invited to her graduation party that will take place in Nimos hotel immediately after the ceremony on Campus.

Dr. Nene Buji: *(Regretfully)* Congratulation Yune, I wish I could be there, but I have to rush back to my job. You know how Acirema is, work work work.

Mrs. Yune–Njoya: *(Playfully)* Come to think of it, the rejected stone has become the corner stone. My Lord Chung, the bishop is loyal to Rome, Prof. Mnkong and Justice Noyen work in Arenia, Engineer Nchioh works in Airegin, Nene in Acirema and even though Yaya is here in Kale she works with a British firm I am the one, the rejected stone amongst the six of us who has ended up serving our fatherland. Teachers in Kale toil and sacrifice for nation building but we are the least paid.

We train presidents, Divisional officers and accountants who earn ten times more than us and people say a teacher's reward is in heaven. That is why I am almost giving in to my daughter's desire to go to Acirema.

Dr. Nene Buji: I know that every Kalean parent feels fulfilled when he sends a child to Acirema and every Kalean youth dreams of going to Acirema but the grass is not as green as it looks from a distance. There we are slaves. We work so hard but are not even allowed to invest in our home countries. There is racism, terrorism, all the isms and the natural disasters. I have been there for ten years but nothing to show for. No husband or children. We work and work to produce drugs that sometimes kill more than they cure.

Bishop Chung: (*Cuts in*) It is God that heals

Mrs. Yune–Njoya: (*Surprised*) Acirema is not a heaven? We know that it is the land of impossibilities, the land of milk and honey. Tell me more so that I can educate my daughter and my pupils who believe they can make it only in Acirema.

Justice Noyen: Mnkong won the Acirema lottery but we did not go there. We refused to be enslaved again. Our parents were forced into slavery but today we are lured into it by the lottery. People leave prestigious jobs to go and be bus drivers, shop keepers, barmaids and gas operators in the name of being in Acirema. To them our certificates are never good enough. If Acirema gives you a glass of water then it will confiscate your lakes. They can never give more than they take. Do you know that when there was the civil war in Airegin they sold arms to both the government and the rebels? (*Pauses, then speaks calmly*) Yune, my husband and I work for the Arenia government because one good turn deserves another. Hope you understand what I mean?

Pharmacist Yaya: The Kalean government did not invest in our generation so we owe it no responsibility. I passed the common Entrance in list A, but was not given admission in the government school in Dom because my mother did not bribe the principal. Though I had five papers with twenty-two points in the A level I was not given a scholarship because I am neither from the preferred region nor the daughter of a minister or parliamentarian. When I enrolled in the University the monthly allowance that was given to university students was stopped and school fees introduced. Come to think of it most of those who studied from the 'O' Levels right to PhD on Kalean scholarship are now working in Acirema, United nation and the few that have returned home have joined their parents to siphon the nation's wealth. This nation gave me nothing.

Mrs. Yune–Njoya: This talking will take us nowhere; let us think of ways of developing our village because there is no place like home.

Pharmacist Yaya: Yune you have really changed. You are now mature and very patriotic

Mrs. Yune–Njoya: Besides the fact that experience is the best teacher, we need to be better than our leaders whom we criticized.

Prof Mnkong: (Nodding his head) that is an excellent idea Yune. I think we should create a development fund for our village.

Dr. Nene Buji: I think we should instead create an NGO; that way those of us in the Diaspora can easily sought for funds for the development of the village.

Engr. Nchioh: That is an excellent proposal. Let us toast for development and for friendship (*They toast happily*). If you don't mind I will constitute a file for the NGO so that we look at it in a week.

Justice Noyen: No problem. I let us identify the projects that our NGO will handle.

Mrs. Yune–Njoya: (*Excited*) that is good. We need community oriented projects. I suggest we begin with health. Our hospitals lack personnel, equipment and drugs.

Dr. Nene Buji: That will be easy to handle. I just need to contact hospitals abroad. You know as they advanced they look for where to throw their obsolete equipment that are still useful to us.

Justice Noyen: We need good roads too.

Mrs. Yune–Njoya: Don't go there, the government does not allow her citizens to do road

Justice Noyen: We will do that through the council.

Prof. Mnkong: That is an excellent idea if the money will not end in private pockets.

Engr.Nchioh: Prof. Let us do our part because no crime will go unpunished.

Mrs. Yune-Njoya: We also need to set up a fund for the education of the girl child. Girl children should be educated not only to become lawyers, pharmacists and Engineers but to preserve their virtuous and emulate our mothers who knew that the fate of the nation is anchored on them.

All: (*Clap for Yune*)

Dr. Nene Buji: I suggest Yaya and Yune should take charge of the affairs of the NGO. We should leave our phone numbers and emails so that the document will be forwarded to us. An account should also be created to enable us contribute and sought for funds.

Mrs. Yune-Njoya: We will do our best and the sky will be our Limit. I already have a small scholarship scheme for underprivileged girls in our village. Now we will include all needy children.

Dr. Nene Buji: As we were discussing I texts some of my colleagues and they are ready to support in cash and in kind.

Engr. Nchioh: That is the spirit, action now now.

The End

Printed in the United States
By Bookmasters